To

____

From:

____

Date:

____

Published by TLC Publishing Company
Brandywine, MD 20613

Transformational Lifestyle Coloring
Adult Coloring Book

ISBN 978-1646690251-1

Disclaimer
The purpose of this book is to introduce an activity that allowsindividuals to relax and de-stress, and tap into their creativity. The author or publisher does not guarantee that this activity will release any or all stress, help to relax, or restore. The author and publisher shall have neither liability nor responsibility to anyone with respect to any loss or damage caused, or alleged to be caused directly or indirectly by the information contained in this journal.

www.tawawn.com

Transformational Lifestyle Coloring

Coloring books are no longer just for children. In fact, coloring for adults is the craze these days – and for good reason. Adults worldwide are rediscovering the beauty in the childhood joy of sitting down with a coloring book and a box of color pencils. They are learning that coloring has many benefits that contribute to calming the mind, de-stressing, reducing anxiety, and contributing to their overall mental and emotional well-being.

Research has shown that adult coloring has a de-stressing effect. It helps to calm anxiety. It allows the amygdala (fear center) of your brain to relax. Coloring is a mental exercise that allows you to focus on a particular activity, provide comfort, peace, temporarily free you from the day-to-day pressures of life, and lets you tap into your imagination and to become more creativity.

As a consultant, and certified life coach, I truly believe that apart of becoming your best self, and creating your best life requires you to engage in activities that contributes to your self-care. This is why I created the Transformational Lifestyle Coloring – Adult Coloring Books. It has been specifically designed as a therapeutic tool for adults to unwind, relax, be creative, and escape to a place of serenity for emotional mental restoration.

Are you ready to de-stress, have fun, and just get lost in colors?

All you have to do is grab your color pencil, choose your colors, and start coloring between the lines, or maybe even outside the line.

Benefits of Adult Coloring

What once was an activity that kept as many of us entertained as children, is now resurfacing as a trend adults are coming to love.

The therapeutic elements parents sought to keep their children calm or entertained are now being applied to adults, to help distract them from the daily pressures of life.

.

Let me share the top 7 benefits of coloring for adults:

1. Your brain experiences relief by entering a meditative state

2. Stress and anxiety levels have the potential to be lowered

3. Negative thoughts are expelled as you take in positivity

4. Focusing on the present helps you achieve mindfulness

5. Unplugging from technology promotes creation over consumption

6. Coloring can be done by anyone, not just artists or creative types

7. It's a hobby that can be taken with you wherever you go

GRAB YOUR CRAYONS AND COLOR PENCILS